The Lafaya Way®

A Fresh Approach to Parenting Hypersensitive Children

Lafaya Mitchell, LMFT

Co-Published by
Leverage Press/Hybrid Global Publishing
301 E 57th Street, 4th Floor
New York, NY 10022

Manufactured in the United States of America, or in the United Kingdom when distributed elsewhere.

Author Lafaya Mitchell, LMFT

The Lafaya Way®

A Fresh Approach to Parenting Hypersensitive Children

ISBN: 978-1-948181-10-5

Cover Design by: Cynthia Lay
Interior Design: Leverage Press

Dedication

This book is dedicated to my motivating and inspiring support team. Thank you all for believing in me so much that it inspired me to believe in myself.

James Mitchell my love, my life, my light. You are my best friend, my other, my forever favorite. Your patience and never-ending love inspires me to be a better me. Thank you for being my partner, my strength, my editor, and anything else that I need you to be. I love you to infinity and beyond.

To my 3 beautiful children, every

day you are all an inspiration to me. You all have the most magnificent hearts holding a love unmatched by anything else in my life. Your fantastic smiles and the purity of your laughter are the most wonderful sights and sounds available in this world. I love you all to the moon and back.

Acknowledgements

To Christyna Giles-Washington for your sisterhood, love, support, and prayers. You continue to teach me what it means to LIVE true to our queendom status. I love you sis.

To Lovell Bolden, my Irish twin, for always believing in and supporting your big sister. Words can't express how much you encourage me. My sister love knows no bounds for you.

To Dr. Shira Bush for putting up with my bratty ways, my many run-on sentences, and stubborn frustration when asked to be more concise with the things I say.

You transformed the message I had inside of me into a wonderful, easy to understand tool that will be used to help many frustrated parents and support people around the world.

Special thanks to the many brave parents I have had the privilege to work with. Your courage knows no bounds. I truly appreciate all that you have taught me over the years. This book would not have been possible without you.

Table of Contents

Preface

This book belongs to parents who wish to more effectively parent children with challenges. My unique philosophy, The Lafaya Way is an advanced relational approach utilizing "true" authenticity to achieve positive interactions based on the deeply rooted human desire to feel understood and validated.

It offers a fresh perspective on how to achieve effective results with hypersensitive children. Hypersensitive children are abnormally impacted by certain stimuli that neurotypical children are not normally sensitive to.

The Lafaya Way amplifies the importance of an enlightened (deeper) understanding of one's own and others truest intentions, thus increasing the likelihood that you will respond in ways that will reinforce getting both your own and your child's needs met. Following The Lafaya Way, decreases strong emotional reactivity and increases the likelihood of cooperative interactions.

The Lafaya Way parenting book series is for parents who have misbehaving, difficult to reach hypersensitive children.

Originally, I named the book series

"Raising Asp-Holes." My intention for that title was to give parents' permission to admit how tough it is to raise children with Aspie-like traits (will define Aspie-like traits later). Some people were offended by that title. It is my goal to reach and change as many lives as possible with the valuable information contained within this book series, so The Lafaya Way, it is!

Warning!

My particular brand of assistance does not come without a price. I know some of you may be thinking "Ok, now what? Haven't I already paid enough?" If you are reading this book, the answer is no!

The initial price to pay that is being asked of you is to put aside your pride and defensive attitude. The Lafaya Way offers the guidance necessary to "truly" set aside that pride and defensiveness. This can be especially challenging when dealing with what I lovingly call a little "Asp-hole."

I coined the term "Asp-hole," because I wanted to get to the truth about the experience of raising hypersensitive children with Aspie (Asperger's Disorder) traits.

You may discover that many of the traits that cause social problems for the Aspie kid as identified in Chapter 4 of this book may also be commonly found in other disorders such as Autism Spectrum, ADHD, Reactive Attachment Disorder, moderate to severe Mood/Anxiety Disorders, and Emotional Disturbance diagnoses. These Aspie traits also add clarity to the reasoning behind my use of the term "Asp-hole" throughout this book.

This book focuses on the results you achieve with hypersensitive children whose appropriate functioning is disrupted due to social, emotional, and/or behavioral issues. You will learn the foundational requirements for building a better relationship with your hypersensitive, difficult-to-reach child.

Introduction

Before we get started, I have good news and bad news for you.

The good news is that we are all powerful beyond our imagination and regaining charge over your home is closer than you think. For most of the parents whom I have seen over the years, especially those who have gone through the terrible ordeal of learning and trying some of the more popular techniques offered such as Dialectical Behavioral Therapy (DBT) and Applied Behavioral Analysis (ABA) and discovering their child is still failing to react in functionally appropriate ways, your situation is not as hopeless as you think. The Lafaya Way philosophy offers the slight adjustments and alterations you must make to achieve improved relations and interactions with your tough-to-deal-with children.

The bad news is that the journey requires exploration of why things impact you the way they do and active participation on your part to change the way you think, feel, and respond to your challenges. As a parent, it is essential to eliminate the habit of blaming, shaming, and "guilting" both yourself and your child in order to achieve the desired positive results. It can be a difficult journey for you to gain access to your innate parental strength.

Now again, you may be asking yourself, "What strength?" My goal is to empower you with information on how to combat feelings of disempowerment, in addition to instructing you how to exercise your personal power to improve your life and that of your child.

The largest encouraging factor for writing this book is my mission to restore and promote hope, healing and freedom to families who have been searching for an answer for gaining positive results for their difficult-to-manage child.

Throughout the years, I have accomplished this goal with the parents whom I have had the honor to work with.

Chapter 1
How I Got Started

*"Progress consists largely
of learning to apply laws and truths
that have always existed."*

-John Allan May

Over 20 years ago while still in college, I worked for an in-home care service for developmentally disabled adult violent males and/or sex offenders. I learned early on that I had a knack for persuading those residents who seemed to be a bit more resistant to do anything requested of them.

During those humble beginnings, I learned the benefit of having a non-judgmental and calm internal presence, which assisted me in my ability to de-escalate residents quickly while eliciting compliance and engagement faster than my fellow residential counselors.

I have always had a strong desire to be as helpful as possible when counseling others. Making a positive difference in the lives of those I work with is the #1 reason I do what I do.

I moved on to work with Severely Emotionally Disturbed (SED) children in the foster care system. These particular children were labeled behaviorally unfit to stay in traditional foster homes and were placed in residential treatment centers.

According to the staff, I obtained exemplary behavior and compliance from children who were the most difficult-to-manage.

My success was largely due to my calm internal presence in this environment.

Early on, I learned that these previously abused or neglected children, often labeled as hypervigilant (what I call hypersensitive to how others are responding), required a calm presence. If the professional feared a meltdown, then one was almost sure to occur fairly quickly from the child. I have witnessed the breakdown of order each time an anxious or agitated staff member would attempt to deal with these hypersensitive children.

Please understand, this is not a slap in the face to the individuals who work with challenging children. I have acquired the necessary wisdom to producing better results when working with your not-so-typical behaviorally challenged child or adult.

My Work with ASD and Other Difficult-to-Manage Disorders

Thirteen years ago, I began intensive outpatient level work with children who were either recently released from hospitalization or had failed traditional therapy for many years and were assessed with the need for a higher level of care than traditional therapy can provide.

The Intensive Outpatient (IOP) level of treatment requires a commitment of a minimum of 3 days per week, 3 hours per day of therapy. When I was introduced to this treatment program, I primarily worked with children diagnosed on the Autism Spectrum. At that time, I knew very little about the Autism Spectrum Disorder (ASD) diagnosis. Therefore, I needed to learn as much as I could about ASD. Immediately, I learned there wasn't much information and/or tangible techniques for working with ASD children.

In addition, after some time working with children on the Spectrum, I discovered that some of the information available describing the experiences of children diagnosed with Autism was erroneous. If I was going to be effective in my work with children on the Spectrum, I needed to figure it out independently.

Chapter 2

First Encounter as an
ASD Counselor

*"A problem cannot be solved
at the level of consciousness
in which it occurs."*

-Albert Einstein

First Case Study: "Blue Tunnel Boy"

The first case assigned to me was a child who had been identified as being on the "low" end of the Spectrum. He seemed like the "textbook definition" of Autism.

He appeared completely wrapped up in his own world, on his own agenda, and unable to respond to the experiences of others. This child didn't even answer to being called by his own name, unless he was being offered something he wanted. I knew I had my work cut out for me and was uncertain if I was up for the task.

Initially, we had had sessions, which I attempted to get him to engage, which only seemed to annoy the crap out of him since I was disrupting his isolated play. He ignored me, sometimes taking the time to angrily grunt at me. I couldn't even get the child to look in my direction.

After several frustrating sessions, I recognized that he really liked a 4' light blue accordion folding tunnel. He would often "misuse" the tunnel by picking it up, putting it over his head and body for a minute and then tossing it to the side to grab his next toy of interest.

I often felt like he'd put the tunnel on just to try to escape my attempts to get him to engage. I really didn't know what to do with him; this child didn't even respond to his own mother.

One day, in a fit of desperation, I decided to try to identify with what his experience must have been like, so I picked up the blue tunnel and put it over my own head as I had seen him do many times before. Immediately, I recognized that it was a nice enclosed space that blocked me from seeing anything except the blue, which also kept others from seeing me.

I said aloud, "I see why you like it in here. It's nice, nobody can see me and I can't see anybody." After a few moments of being in the blue tunnel, I pulled the tunnel down to take a peek at what the child was doing. When I pulled down the tunnel, to my surprise, the child was looking directly at me with this very faint look of curiosity on his face (his facial expressiveness was muted). In my mind, I thought he must have been thinking, "What is this crazy lady doing?" Once I realized he was looking at me, I did what I had seen him do several times when he peeked to see if I was still attempting to engage with him and pulled the tunnel back over my head saying, "If I can't see you, you can't see me." After a few seconds, I'd peek again to see if he was still staring at me, and he was, this time with a faint smile in his eyes. This turned into a strange game of peek-a-boo with a 7-year old.

I learned a great lesson that day: if you want to capture the interest and attention of someone on the Spectrum, take an interest in what **THEY** are interested in. This may not be an easy task, especially with children who truly seem to be in their own world or on their own agenda. It is well worth it to open the window of opportunity to be allowed into their world.

After that day, it became incrementally easier for him to allow me to join him in his play. Now mind you, it began with me asking him if I could play the game he was playing and he would throw a toy in front of me and continue his play alone, while turning his back to me. This improved as he played next to me, without turning his back. Then, playtime progressed to us playing together, while then advancing to us taking turns picking the games (all of which were specific to teaching him social skills).

This child was almost completely non-verbal, non-responsive, and isolated when we first met and he grew to be fully verbal, responsive and even showing empathy towards others within six months. This was one of the most rewarding experiences I have ever had working with children on the Autism Spectrum.

Chapter 3
My Personal Experience
as a Parent

*"Life is really what happens to you
while you're making other plans."*

-Dr. Wayne Dyer

Second Case Study: "My Daughter"

My daughter was born with a variety of sensory issues. She did not like eye contact, certain voices, and was overwhelmed by a variety of sounds. When any person, including me, would try to pick her up, look at her and talk to her, she would squirm excessively and then break out into a crying fit if you did not stop.

Two of my close relatives kept saying, "She's just spoiled; she's going to learn how to be okay when we talk to her, we're not doing anything wrong with her."

At that time, I instinctually knew that their assessment was incorrect.

My response was, "If you would like for her not to like you very much, then you can keep up with that attitude. However, if you would like to understand her, you better listen to what she's showing you." She was a newborn baby, so of course, she couldn't speak. Her actions, however, communicated everything we needed to know to help make her comfortable.

The first thing I noticed was that she responded with more irritation to deep voices. Then, I noticed she could not tolerate people talking in her face for more than a couple of seconds and avoided all eye contact. She responded with a great deal of anxiety to loud noises (especially sirens, bells, etc.). I made it my mission to try to figure her out.

I was on a mission to help my baby girl learn to be okay. First, I addressed the aversion to eye contact. I would hold her towards me and look at her for a few seconds, attempting to turn her so that she had to look at me. As soon as she squirmed, I turned her away. When she calmed down, I turned her back towards me and repeated the act. I would go through sessions of this routine with her several times a day and noticed that she was able to stay turned towards me for longer periods of time, before having to be turned away from me.

Applying this no pressure approach, after a while, I could hold her gaze for longer periods of time, until she achieved a "normal" gaze time. Let me be clear that this did not happen in one day. It took time, and the progression was slow and incremental. However, the time that I invested was well worth it.

The next step was to work on her tolerating being spoken to. I practiced the same method as the eye gaze and she responded amazingly. The next task was to work with her on loud noise tolerance. Her sensory issues caused her to tense-up tightly and scream whenever a motorcycle, ambulance, or big truck drove by or even when the doorbell rang.

Again, the same two well meaning, loving family members would say, "Now there is no reason for her to overreact like that just because of some noise." Again, I found myself correcting them by saying, "She is quite obviously, genuinely afraid of and sensitive to these sounds, and judging her for it is definitely not going to help." I did not know how to help her with the sound sensitivity at that time, and felt bad for the torture she seemed to experience during loud sounds.

It wasn't until she was about age 2 that I was able to use language to help her. One day, a motorcycle passed by and I watched her almost jump out of her skin as she usually did and rev up to cry. I jumped up with her, held my ears and exclaimed, "I don't like that sound!" She stopped in her tracks, looked at me a bit puzzled and repeated, "I don't like that sound" and covered her ears. I nodded to her with the same fearful look that she was giving me, while covering my ears and saying, "Yeah, I don't like that sound, it's too loud." After this, it took a little time and some practice as opportunities arose, however, the strong reactivity to loud noises became a thing of the past.

In that situation, I helped her verbalize what was causing her extreme physical and emotional reaction, while assisting her to learn how to regulate herself better through the experience. Most importantly, I never judged her for how she reacted. I did not expect her nor want her to behave like a child whom she wasn't, and I worked diligently to help her get on the path to proper functionality through effective avenues.

This is exactly what I am hoping to teach you to do with your child.

Learn to accept them for who they are, eliminate any judgment and work with them according to their personal ability.

Chapter 4
ASD: Common Disruptive Traits

"Human beings are primarily emotional creatures who often operate in irrational ways...
Expecting humans to behave logically all the time is like expecting machines to feel emotion."

-Steven Siebold

My experience has taught me that some of the most misunderstood, mistreated, and mismanaged children are those diagnosed with Asperger's (Aspie).

Asperger's has been identified as a diagnosis along the disorders of the Autism Spectrum. These children are often what I call "passers," meaning they can look as if they are perfectly normal and often act difficult, defiant, and want to have their way. These children don't tend to have the "low IQ" often associated with children on the lower end of the Spectrum. In reality, these children's IQ tests are nowhere near accurate because the lower end of ASD children generally refuse to participate in the testing process because it's meaningless to them. Aspie children often have higher intelligence and are socially awkward. This makes them sometimes very difficult to identify to the untrained eye and often leaves them vulnerable to a great deal of abuse because they don't look "disordered."

They are most often susceptible to being bullied by other students and tend to have extremely low self-esteem due to failed attempts to fit in. Furthermore, they suffer unintentional mistreatment by their parents and other authority figures due to the perception that they are being defiant or selfish through their behaviors.

Common Disruptive Aspie-Like Traits

1. Lacks empathy (even sometimes appears to get extreme enjoyment out of annoying the hell out of others);

2. Often on their own agenda (only want to do what they want to do without much concern about what others want or how others feel);

3. Difficulty reading social cues or not responding to those cues in socially appropriate ways;

4. Hyper-focused in areas of interest (they may want to spend all day talking about one subject that interests them);

5. Concrete (black and white) thinkers; frequently they are moral giants when it comes to the wrongdoing of others;

6. Often have some variation ranging from mild to severe sensory issues (including sensitivities to sounds, tastes, textures, tactile sensations, sights); and

7. Difficulty sequencing – they are often unable to arrange things in order (e.g., the child may not be able to easily order things as

simple as understanding that when they run out of shampoo, the next step is to inform the parent to get more shampoo).

Difficulty sequencing can also occur when the child is asked to clean out their closet and the task may seem overwhelming to them because they cannot sequence the order of how to go about it. A neurotypical ("normally" functioning) child would know to first remove the clothes from the closet floor, hang up the pants and dresses, fold their undershirts and underwear, and place them into the drawers. Aspie kids often cannot easily sequence this way.

Aspie children have a unique set of challenges, which often contribute to their extreme difficulty navigating their social world and eventually resulting in anxiety associated with social interaction and behavioral/emotional issues.

The above set of symptomology is what often creates what I refer to as an Asp-hole. I'll leave the understanding of that terminology up to your imagination.

Chapter 5

The Lafaya Way

Know Yourself,
Know Your Child

*"When you move from
thinking to awareness, thinking
becomes more productive."*

-Inspired by the Teachings of
Eckhart Tolle

The Lafaya Way philosophy's primary focus is to decrease and/or eliminate the detrimental effects of an occurrence that I've coined "emotion-soaking."

Emotion-soaking is the unintentional sponging of the internal experiences (deep down feelings) of the person(s) one is interacting with. Emotion-soaking happens for most human beings on some level. For example, feeling upset when another person is angry with you is a common occurrence in human interactions.

In reference to emotion-soaking in difficult-to-manage children, the goal is to address the unique challenges that hinder the ability to obtain effective results (conducive to passable social functioning) with hypersensitive children.

Hypersensitivity is defined as mild to severe sensitivity to everyday environmental elements that annoy some individuals more than others and interfere with their ability to perceive and/or concentrate.

For children with disruptions in functioning, which meet the symptomology requiring a mental health diagnosis, hypersensitivity can render them extremely difficult to deal with, especially for parents and those who work with them consistently. For children on the Autism Spectrum, including Asperger's Disorder, some of their hypersensitivity is often referred to as sensory issues.

For the hypersensitive individual, the effects of emotion-soaking can cause extreme reactivity when another individual is upset. With over a decade of experience that I've had working successfully with Autism Spectrum Disorder (ASD), I have learned the emotion-soaking phenomenon is often present in moderate to severe degrees.

The Lafaya Way was developed

to address those emotion-soaking, exaggerated behaviors/responses that did not change with the use of other methods such as Cognitive-Behavioral Therapy (CBT), Dialectical Behavioral Therapy (DBT), Applied Behavioral Analysis (ABA), Nurtured Heart Approach alone.

I support utilizing the methods mentioned above since they can be effective for most neurotypical children. However, for children with unique challenges, especially children with moderate to severe hypersensitivity, popular methods such as CBT, DBT, and ABA alone are often ineffective.

The Lafaya Way addresses the missing links in those methods by tackling the areas that need to be addressed by the parent(s) personally; a soul searching if you will.

The primary goal of The Lafaya Way is to teach parents and others who work with difficult-to-manage children how to make their internal experiences match the appropriate external reactions in order to create a safer environment for the "sensitive" child to utilize learned coping skills.

The Lafaya Way is a key to unlocking barriers to challenging individuals with strong emotion-soaking reactivity by utilizing two primary components:

1. Know yourself; and
2. Know your child.

The first portion of The Lafaya Way two-component process takes into account the following "hidden issues" of parents:

1. Not knowing themselves well enough; and
2. Not recognizing the impact of how their "internal experiences" effect their hypersensitive child.

Component 1 - Know Yourself

In order for The Lafaya Way to work effectively, parents must take a hard and honest look at themselves and their unintentional contributions provoking unhealthy/unwanted responses from their children. As parents, you must make the internal changes necessary to minimize your provocations. The key is being open to and engaging in personal-growth activities and proper self-care.

Personal Growth

As a parent of a hypersensitive child, develop a logical way of interacting/communicating both verbally and non-verbally with your child in order to reduce the effects of emotion-soaking. As a parent/caregiver, identify what your authentic internal and external experiences are and some of the possible reasons for such experiences. The internal experiences often result from:

- Your past experiences;
- Incongruence between your truest intentions and your actual reactions; and
- Unfruitful wishing or idealizing a false child (expecting/desiring your child to be someone he/she is not).

1. Past Experiences

Past experiences can contribute to

fears and frustrations impacting your ability to make fitting decisions when faced with difficult situations, due in some part to trying to be less like your parents.

Past experiences can hinder your ability to say "no" for the necessity of self-care. Many parents, who feel they have been deprived of things they desired from their own parents, often, fight an internal battle when faced with similar circumstances. This is prevalent in situations where parents must hold back things from their children because he/she hasn't earned the privilege to receive them.

For example, when a child who has

been rude to their parent asks for a toy and the parent is upset when he/she must say no because the parent feels the child hasn't been kind or respectful.

The parent who experiences anger when they tell their child "no" and feels the need to justify their "no" is not responding with the logical consequences of "when you are not nice all day, you do not get rewards." The offended parent instead often responds according to the background anger-making thoughts, which scream, "if you would just do what you are supposed to do, I'd be happy to get you what you want when I am able."

The difference maker is the emotion behind the "no." If you see it as a logical consequence, there is not much emotion attached. However, if you feel upset about saying no, there are other personal (usually connected to past experiences) reasons attached to your anger, contributing to more negative responses from both you and your child.

On the other end of the continuum are parents who know full well that the child hasn't earned a privilege and say "yes" when they should be saying "no." This is a set up for the parent to feel bitter and resentful later on when the child continues to mistreat them.

The inappropriate "yes" also reinforces the negative behavior the child has been participating in, giving the child the message that he/she can act out and still get whatever they want.

2. Incongruence Between Your Truest Intentions and Your Actual Reactions

It is important to first understand that any action taken against one's truest intention is an action against one's self. People often lose sight of their core values in their relationships, family, etc., especially during difficult interactions.

Most of the time, people desire peace, safety, love, and happiness for themselves and their families. However, during conflict, there is a strong tendency to engage in behaviors that work directly against obtaining these desires.

Those who choose to engage in sabotaging behaviors that work against their core goals often become resentful and bitter and blame either themselves or whomever they are interacting with.

A snowball effect occurs during difficult interactions, followed by bitterness, resentment, and blame.

The pattern repeats itself until it balloons into a huge, catastrophic dilemma that has the potential to roll over and destroy anything in its path.

For example, you want your child to feel safe, loved, and cared for and you find yourself judging them, putting them down, or lacking acceptance for who they are; these approaches work directly against your goal to have your child feel safe, loved, and cared for.

Children who feel misunderstood, judged and put down feel the opposite of safe, loved and cared for; they often feel out of control, hated by others, and see themselves as a burden on their parents and family.

On the same note, when your child foundationally wants to be loved and accepted, when they do things to hinder others from potentially liking them, they are working against themselves.

The desire to be liked by others is often not verbalized by children with difficulties. On many occasions, the children may even say they don't care whether people like them; the proof of their desire to be liked or loved is found in their anger and depression from not being liked. The children's actions speak their truth, as they are often unable to verbalize their "real truth."

As a parent, it is important to recognize your child's misbehavior (especially if it causes you to be upset with them) as a form of self-harm to the child. They are actually hurting themselves by causing others to dislike them through their misbehavior.

This new understanding can trigger your parental protection to kick in, meaning that you will come from your protective place to do all you can to keep your child from hurting himself.

Most parents do intend to protect their child, however, they come from the unsafe space that screams; "You are pissing me off, why won't you choose to do better?" Instead of the safer space of, "You are hurting yourself when you cause others to dislike you. Let me help you get to a better place."

3. Unfruitful Wishing or Idealizing a False Child

Wishing that the one you love would behave as someone else demonstrates a lack of acceptance for who "they" are and blocks the ability to show unconditional love. I strongly urge you to "let go" of the image you dreamt of for your child.

Instead, embrace, encourage, and enhance his/her strengths.

Self-Care

A large emphasis is placed on the importance of parental and caregiver self-care and personal growth work to create a healthy mind/body/spirit connection. People who do not treat themselves well, rarely feel they are getting their needs met. Therefore, good self-care leads to better results and establishing positive relationships.

The lack of self-care blocks the ability to show unconditional love. If you do not feel taken care of by your "self," you will most likely not feel cared for by others. Thus, leading to a lack of energy to put into loving others.

Component 2 - Know Your Child

Changing your internal experience (to change what you present underneath your external verbal communication to your emotion-soaking child) is also assisted by:

- Gaining an understanding of the child's specific challenges and how those challenges manifest. This will reduce unfruitful expectations, thus eliminating parental blame and shameful thoughts; and

- Setting aside your pride and focusing more on validating your child's experiences.

One common area of confusion and difficulty for parents is failing to acknowledge that their children with sensory issues cannot help having strong reactions to certain stimuli that may not affect others in an upsetting way. It is important not to react to the initial embarrassment or irritation you may feel when your child acts in a way that appears exaggerated.

I have heard countless stories from parents expressing how embarrassed they were when their children did things such as gag when trying new foods, panic while in crowds or break out in a screaming fit when a dog would start barking.

Parents often make the mistake of perceiving their child's reaction as an overreaction, which can often contribute to the child feeling invalidated. This may fuel feelings of self-hatred in the child because he/she may feel weird from being uncommonly affected by things "normal people" aren't impacted by.

- Identify disruptive, inappropriate, non-beneficial external reactions and how they are often inconsistent with core goals and/or incongruent with internal experiences (giving confusing/mixed messages and triggering unwanted behaviors from the frustrated child); and

• Adapt and respond according to your understanding and newfound empathy for your child's experiences. Adapting to your individual child's needs often requires "thinking outside the box." A favorite joke of mine is, "Boxes are made for squares."

Note: For a more in-depth discussion on unfruitful wishing, self-care, and other know yourself or know your child concepts, please read the third book in The Lafaya

Way series, "Becoming the True Parental You."

Chapter 6
The "Core4" Steps
of The Lafaya Way

"Change your beliefs;
change your feelings.
Nothing that another person
does can affect you.
Only you can create damage
by creating negative emotion
in reaction to their actions."

-Louise Hay

The "Core 4" Steps of The Lafaya Way®

Step 1: Remain Calm

1. Understand the Impact of
   Emotion-Soaking

Understand that your child is often reacting to the underlying frustration manifested by you and not exclusively to the words coming out of your mouth.

If you are trying to sound calm when you are not internally calm, it is confusing and upsetting to concrete thinkers. It is more effective to take a moment, focus on problem solving and match your internal feelings to your external behavior and/or language.

2. Avoid Personalizing Your Child's Behavior

Keep in mind the child is likely to be sensitive to and/or experience difficulty navigating through perceived negative stimulation.

In order to help build a trusting relationship with your child it is necessary to recognize when their reactions originate from "sensitivities" and not from the fact that they are spoiled and/or do not "like you."

Do not get wrapped up in the

misperception that your child appears to dislike you or worse yet, is too much of a "brat" to engage.

Please remember your child's behavior is most often "not about you" nor about him/her being a "bad seed."

Misbehavior often has more to do with your child's sensitivities and the protective space they move into, in order to ward off undesirable feelings connected to strong reactions to stimulation.

Do not personalize your child's behavior.

Understanding the real reasons for your child's behavior and remaining diligent to avoid personalizing their behaviors strengthens your ability to maintain a "true" calm.

Had I personalized blue tunnel boy's behavior (chapter 2 case study), it would have become more about me trying so hard to be liked and his lack of cooperation than about the real truth; he was more comfortable alone than he was trying to interact with others. The personalized line of thinking would have lessened the likelihood of effective problem solving, which occurred only when I put myself in his shoes.

Personalizing my daughter's avoidant behavior (Chapter 3 Case Study) would have likely yielded the results I see repeatedly with families of children with sensitivities. The parents feel resentful, unappreciated and mistreated, and the child feels misunderstood, guilty, and angry.

Step 2: Find Their "Real" Truth

Put yourself in an empathetic role by asking yourself the following questions:

1. How does my child feel? Ask this question without judging how they feel or comparing their feelings to others'.

2. How does it benefit my child

to respond in a certain way? Ask
yourself this question and consider
that it harms the child more and
keeps them from getting their
needs met when their reasons
appear to be manipulative.

Perceived manipulation makes you
upset and creates an atmosphere
where the child does not get his/her
needs met. Adjust your perception
to see manipulation as self-harm, to
prevent yourself from becoming
indignant towards your child's
apparent manipulation.

3. If I were my child, how would I
    want to be taught to adapt/adjust?

Would you want someone yelling at

you or being angry with you as they taught you, or would you want them to be more loving and helpful?

Once you have your answer, respond to the child accordingly.

Case Study: Blue Tunnel Boy

An example of applying the three questions suggested above:

1. How did the child feel?

   <u>Plausible Answer:</u> He appeared uncomfortable when being spoken to.

2. How does it benefit the child to respond in the way that he does?

<u>Plausible Answer:</u> When he covers himself with the tunnel, he muffles out those who are looking at him and the sounds of them talking to him (avoiding negative stimulation).

3. How would I want to be taught to adapt/adjust if I were him?

<u>Plausible Answer:</u> Kindly, gently, without judgment, and in the most fun way possible.

Putting Myself in their Shoes

Remember, I mentioned in Chapter 2, in a fit of desperation, I tried to identify with the blue tunnel boy. I picked up the blue tunnel and put it over my head as I immediately, recognized that it was a nice enclosed space that blocked me from seeing anything except the blue, which also kept others from seeing me.

I said to him, "I see why you like it in here. It's nice, nobody can see me and I can't see anybody."

Understanding the "real" truth requires that you ask yourself the questions that allow you to acquire empathetic understanding of your child's experiences.

Step 3: Find Your "Real" Truth

Ask yourself, what is my goal?

Often, a parent's truest desire is to create a better situation for their child and to help their child feel safe, loved, and happy.

Your intended goals may also include empowering your child and contributing to the child's personal growth and ability to function well in society.

Your goal is not to:

- Further frustrate your child by reacting negatively to his/her actions or by judging;

- Contribute to lower self-esteem in your child by putting him/her down; and

- Cause your child to feel misunderstood by invalidating his/her feelings.

When your child feels you are on his/her side, he/she is more likely to respond positively. Please be warned that if the child is feeling like you are on their side, it does not always mean they will respond positively. However, it will increase the likelihood for your child to do as you ask.

Think about it as a means to an end: you are seeking compliant behavior. The expectation for a good attitude to accompany your child's compliance is just a mere

set-up for you to become upset.
Most people are not "happy" doing
things, they don't like to do; we are
just better at "faking it" compared to
our difficult-to-manage children.
The brutal honesty that comes from
little "Asp-holes" is refreshing to
witness.

Emphatically expressing both
verbally and non-verbally your
understanding of what the
hypersensitive child is experiencing,
helps you align with your child and
gain their trust. Gently move the
hypersensitive child into a space of
functionality. Questions to ask
yourself regarding this process are:

1. How do I help desensitize my hypersensitive child from the stimuli that produces a negative reaction in a way that helps my child feel understood?

2. Can I break the things I do to desensitize my child into bite-sized pieces so my sensitive child does not feel overwhelmed?

Case Study: My Daughter's Desensitization in Action

Remember with my daughter, I first addressed the aversion to eye contact. I held her towards me and looked at her for a few seconds, attempting to turn her so that she had to look at me. As soon as she squirmed, I would turn her away. When she calmed down, I would turn her back towards me. I repeatedly practiced multiple sessions of this routine with her several times a day. I noticed she was able to stay turned towards me for longer periods of time before having to be turned away from me.

With this "no pressure" approach, after a while, I held her gaze for increasing periods of time, until she was able to achieve a "normal" gaze time.

Step 4: Reflect and Reinforce

Enjoy the incremental positive

results and allow the small step
changes to increase your faith in the
possibility for positive changes.
Reinforce the positive results and
seek more.

Building **HOPE** raises parental self-
esteem and the self-esteem of your
child, freeing both of you to more
confidently engage in positive
interactions.

Avoiding Potential Potholes (APPs)

Be careful not to judge the speed of
the progress, otherwise you may fall
into a pothole. Recognize and
celebrate the small changes and
improve your outlook. It will also
improve your child's confidence

and reinforce further improvement.

Case Study: My Daughter

Let me be clear that her changes did not occur in one day-the progression was slow and incremental. However, my invested time was well worth it.

Case Study: Blue Tunnel Boy

After that day, it became incrementally easier for him to allow me to join him in his play. Now mind you, it began with me asking him if I could play the game he was playing and he threw a toy in front of me, continuing his play alone while turning his back to me. This improved as he played next to me without turning his back, then we played together, and eventually took turns picking the games (all of which were specific to teaching him social skills).

Remember that this child was almost completely non-verbal, non-responsive, and isolated when we first met. With time and effort, he grew to be fully verbal, responsive and even showing empathy towards others within six months.

Through the relational approach identified in The Lafaya Way, you are seeking to first understand your hypersensitive child's reactions.

Then, you respond in a non-personalizing way (both internally and externally), adapting your responses to what will be most helpful to promote incrementally more functional responses in the sensitive child.

Lastly, reinforce and patiently look forward to the small step improvements.

Chapter 7

Avoiding Potential Potholes
(APPs)

"Give light, and the darkness will disappear of itself."

-Desiderius Erasmus

When you learn how to handle your emotions and make a calm request using different dynamics (external and internal experiences being congruent) and the child still responds with a screaming fit, it's usually because the novelty hasn't worn off. The novelty not wearing off can be a common occurrence in hypersensitive children.

Defining the experience of the novelty not wearing off:

When the child is presented with a current situation that has any similarity to a past occurrence, involving strong negative emotions, the child will be triggered as if the same thing that happened in the past is happening again.

For example, homework time can be one of the most difficult areas to tackle. There may have been many communication mistakes made by everyone involved. If homework time has been an area of struggle, the child may revert back to his/her old habits of interaction even though your way of approaching the situation has changed. It is almost like a **PTSD** (Post Traumatic Stress Disorder) type of response in the child. In order to combat this **PTSD** type of response, the parent needs to bring this reaction to the child's attention.

When you recognize your child's reactions are similar to previous reactions, say to your child, "I know that in the past, homework time was hard and that I, as your mom/dad, made mistakes during that time. However, we have learned new ways to interact so let's both work together to be able to respond better to each other. What can I do to help you?"

(Wait for them to answer first).

If the child can't come up with anything productive, offer suggestions of their best coping skills/methods (i.e. would it be helpful to jump on a trampoline or engage in some other activity to release some stress before starting their work?) Don't forget to validate that it is tough to start/re-start something, but quite possible to accomplish.

Language to Use During Other Pothole Moments

"I know that we have had a difficult time in the past regarding you cleaning your room. I apologize for yelling at you previously. But now that I have learned a better way to make my requests, I hope you feel better about our interaction."

"Sometimes we all have a difficult time with the "novelty wearing off.""

Since I yelled at you in the past, you may still feel at times that I'm yelling at you even though that's not my intention. In the future, don't forget that you have a tough time with the novelty wearing off so remember that can be a possibility when you feel upset."

"Change, even positive changes, can be difficult for you, so if you're extra upset, be aware your struggle with change may be a reason."

One of the best things to do is to explain what is having an impact on the child (if you can figure it out, which should be your first task) in a kind way (best done when the

person speaking is both internally
and externally calm).

Reinforcing Language to Use After a Pothole Moment

"I'm so glad you drew those pictures
for me and were able to express
how you felt in your pictures even
though you couldn't find your words
to express yourself. Drawing can be
a great way for you to release
negative feelings and help calm you
down."

Chapter 8
Conclusion

"Our deepest fear is not that we are inadequate. Our deepest fear is that we are powerful beyond measure.
It is our light, not our darkness that most frightens us...
And as we let our own light shine, we unconsciously give other people permission to do the same.
As we are liberated from our own fear, our presence automatically liberates others."

-Marianne Williamson

The Lafaya Way is the first in a series of books created to help parents navigate through the tough obstacle course to help their children who struggle with social, emotional, and or/behavioral challenges become happy, healthy, and positive contributors to society.

I introduce some of the most difficult to manage traits in socially-challenged children, with a special emphasis on Aspie traits.

The strong effects of the occurrence of emotion-soaking is especially prevalent among children diagnosed with Autism Spectrum Disorder, including Asperger's Syndrome, children diagnosed with moderate to severe mood and anxiety disorders, Reactive Attachment Disorder (RAD), and Attention Deficit Disorders (ADD).

Due to the dramatic impact emotion-soaking has on the hypersensitive child, parents are encouraged throughout this book to take extra steps for personal growth.

Through this work, parents experience internal changes, which assists them to successfully utilize external techniques to achieve a healthier relationship with their difficult-to-manage children.

My goal is to help parents incorporate greater levels of understanding of their own contribution to the negative interactions between them and their child, and better understand what their child is "really" experiencing and why the child may be responding in certain ways.

The Lafaya Way was written to restore hope to parents who have been beaten down by the failure to get good results through techniques (DBT, ABA, etc.) which are often ineffective for some of our most hypersensitive children.

I invite and encourage you to read

The Lafaya Way series in its
entirety. You will discover
additional methods and techniques
to increase empathy in your child,
address tough moments, heal
relationships, and much more.

My hope is to help struggling
parents around the world proudly
say, "With help from The Lafaya
Way, my kid is not such a little
"Asp-hole" after all."

I would love to hear how this advanced relational approach has impacted you and your family's life. Please drop me a note.

Lafaya@pomtsolutions.com

If you would like more education, strategies and techniques to support you in dealing with the behavioral difficulties of your Aspie-trait child, please visit:

www.pomtsolutions.com/media
YouTube@lafayaway.com

To contact Lafaya Mitchell, LMFT for speaking engagements, parent education classes, family sessions, and more, please visit:

www.pomtsolutions.com/contact